Happy Birthday to You!

The MYSTERY BEHIND the

MOST FAMOUS SONG in the WORLD

BY MARGOT THEIS RAVEN · PAINTINGS BY CHRIS SOENTPIET

ACKNOWLEDGMENTS

The author is indebted to the following people and organizations for their invaluable help and research material: The Filson Historical Society, Louisville, Kentucky; The Jefferson County School System Board of Education, Louisville, Kentucky; The Speed Art Museum, University of Louisville, Louisville, Kentucky; The Louisville (Kentucky) Free Public Library, Main Branch; Robert French, founder of the Louisville Academy of Music, Louisville, Kentucky; The Gottesman Libraries, Teachers College, Columbia University, New York, NY; Archives of the Association of Childhood Education International, University of Maryland Libraries, College Park, MD; Dr. Michael Beckerman, Professor and Chair of Music, New York University, New York, NY; researchers Joan Rapp, G. K. Raven, and Gail Petri, Education Resource Specialist, Library of Congress American Memory Learning Page, Washington, D.C. Deep thanks as well to my editor, Aimee Jackson, and to special editor, Judy Gitenstein, who let the story sing its own song.

Sleeping Bear Press®
310 North Main Street, Suite 300
Chelsea, MI 48118
www.sleepingbearpress.com

© 2008 Sleeping Bear Press is an imprint of Gale, a part of Cengage Learning.

Printed and bound in China.

First Edition

10 9 8 7 6 5 4 3 2 1

Library of Congress Cataloging-in-Publication Data

Raven, Margot Theis.
Happy birthday to you! / written by Margot Theis Raven ; illustrated
by Chris K. Soentpiet.
p. cm.
Summary: "In 1889 Patty and Mildred Hill, two Kentucky sisters, wrote the words and composed the melody of "Good Morning to All" for their kindergarten students. They later changed
the words and the song is today known as the happy birthday song"—Provided by publisher.
ISBN 978-1-58536-169-4
1. Hill, Mildred J., 1859-1916. Happy birthday to you—Juvenile literature. 2. Hill, Patty Smith,
1868-1946—Juvenile literature. I. Soentpiet, Chris K. ill II. Title.
ML3930.H56.R38 2008
782.42'158—dc22 2007037438

I magine having a birthday with no one singing the song "Happy Birthday to You." Before the 1900s that's exactly the way things were. You might have had presents, cake, candles, and cards, but there was no Happy Birthday song to sing, because it had not yet been written.

Then once upon a happy day the famous song was born in a children's garden.

   Impossible, you say? Grow a song in a garden? Not impossible at all for a most unusual family that lived in a most unusual home at the time of the Civil War. . . .

One long-ago morning near Louisville, when gas lamps lit rooms and mules pulled street cars, six-year-old Patty Hill gazed in wonder at the tiny bundle of baby and blanket nestled in Mama's arms.

"Meet your little sister," Mama smiled at her little girl with golden-red curls, and at the baby born with the morning, as new to the day as the sun rising to the children's tower-playroom above.

It was a magical place, the tower room overlooking Bellewood, the family's Kentucky home. The tower had eight sides, one for each member of William and Martha Hill's growing family: Papa, Mama, Mildred, Mary, Wallace, Patty, Archibald, and now baby Jessica!

Reverend Hill had built the chapel tower when he founded Bellewood, his school to instruct young women of the South. He believed, most unusually for steamboat days, an educated woman need not marry to have a home.

It was Martha Hill who filled the playroom with boards, boxes, bricks, and barrels for her children to build big dreams. At a time when children were made to work in factories, Martha believed that play was a child's most important work, the way to discover the world.

All day long Martha sang helpful little songs to keep learning and tasks fun, even tasks not so fun! When washing Patty's long curls in a tub, Mama sang:

*down, down, down, daughter,
      down you go—into the water . . .*

Soon Mildred, like Mama, made up little melodies and Patty wrote simple poems.

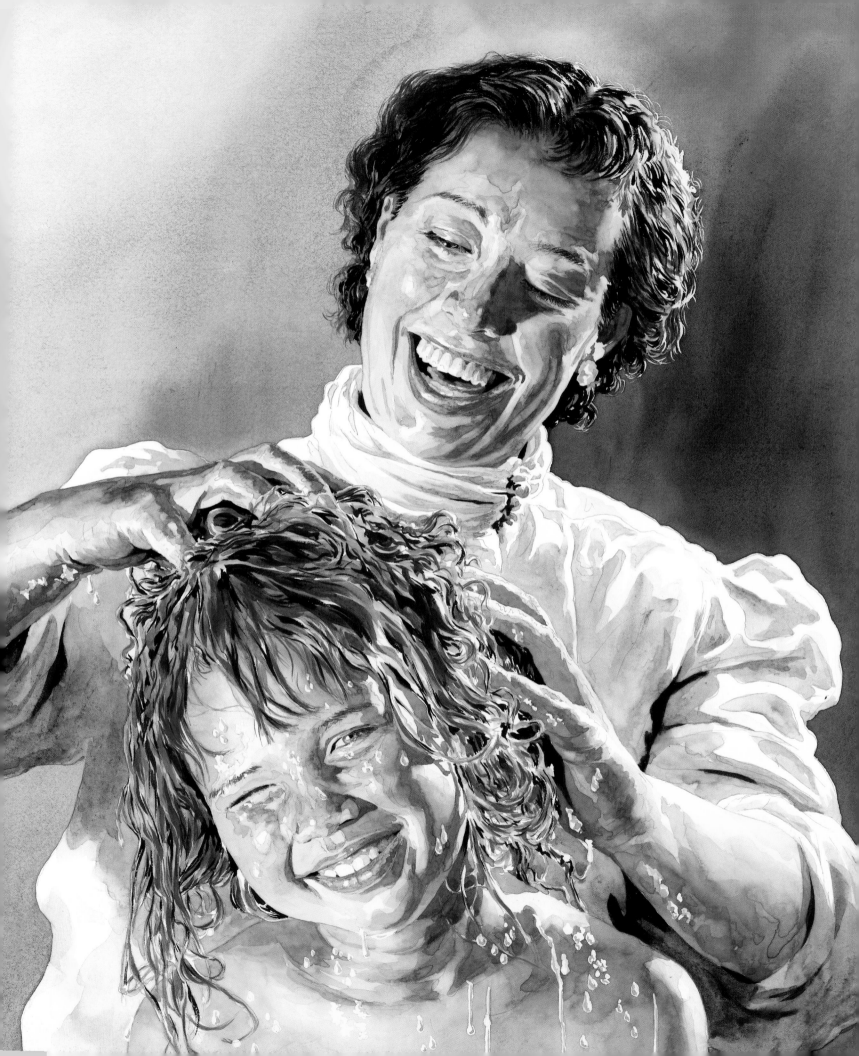

Then one sad day in 1874, not even Mama's songs could dry the children's tears as they said goodbye to Pee Wee, their beloved pony. Pee Wee was off to a new home because the Hill family was leaving Bellewood forever. Reverend Hill was to become president of a college in faraway Missouri.

"Trading memories for new dreams," Martha gently explained to the children as Pee Wee's train pulled away.

Hopes sprouted as high as cornfields in Missouri, until Reverend Hill's health grew frail. One Christmas day the children gave him a book with a ring of stars on a blue cover. "How the stars light the world! How will you light the world when grown?" he asked.

Reverend Hill died too soon to know. Seven heavy hearts returned to Kentucky as lost as coal smoke at night.

"Welcome is the best dish you can serve at the table," Martha sighed, resettling in Louisville in 1878. Like a song without notes, life and the cupboards were empty without Papa.

Martha was nearly penniless. She took in boarders. Blessedly, the children could now finish school.

When Patty graduated she thought of Papa's question: How will you light the world when grown? By now Mildred had become a piano teacher and a talented composer. Patty wondered what *she* might do. Then one day she read a notice in the *Louisville Courier Journal*:

A Free Kindergarten

*Miss Bryan returns to her Kentucky
Home to Instruct Poor Children*

*She will also Train Young Ladies for
Teaching Methods of the Celebrated System*

Patty invited Miss Bryan for tea to hear how Kindergarten was the idea of a German man named Fredrick Froebel. He saw school as a garden—the teacher as the gardener and the children as the flowers that learn best by growing naturally. But what to call this new idea? Not schooling, it was really more like child-gardening. "Kindergarten is the name!" he cried, for *kinder* is German for children.

Patty became the youngest of six students in Louisville's first training class for kindergarten teachers!

Each morning Miss Patty gathered students from poor tenement homes. She washed little hands and faces at school and put children in clean clothes. Then as taught to do, Patty marched the children into a big circle to teach the day's topic. She looked from child to child, until one boy said for all, "Teacher, who are you talking to anyhow?"

Patty then tried the children in smaller groups to learn *their* news. Viola said she couldn't skip very well because her new shoes didn't know how to yet. Tommy was sad because he couldn't find his cookie. But he'd eaten it! Asked to put on her thinking cap, Eloise said, "Not me! I'm putting on my knowing cap."

Patty put on her knowing cap. To teach a child she must reach the child, but the way was through the child's own play. It was the children of Bellewood who built dreams from boards. Mama and Papa added only wise freedom and the help of a little song.

"Eureka!" Patty cried, seeing what was missing for the Kindergarten—songs to teach by play. Patty believed she and Mildred could write songs that kept the child in the music. She wrote four lines to welcome a child to his play-room of friends each morning.

> *Good Morning to you,*
> *Good Morning to you,*
> *Good Morning dear children,*
> *Good Morning to all!*

She asked Mildred to write a melody that was simple and easy enough for any child to sing. But simple was far from easy, Mildred knew. Little voices struggled with notes too high or low. Folk tunes offered a small vocal range, but it was the street sellers' songs — *strawberries like cherries, fresh off the vine* — that filled Mildred's mind with easy tunes doing big work without fuss or fancy.

At night Jessica's young voice tested Mildred's different melodies with Patty's words for her sisters to hear. The next day, the children sang the tunes in school, yet something was still missing.

One night, Mildred, who shared Papa's love of the heavens, met with friends who viewed the sky through telescopes. "Send me some Milky Way!" they laughed when departing. Mildred heard the lightness in their laughter and put the bright notes into her melody. Like stars.

At last her tune formed using simple notes as close as a child's footsteps. It held happiness.

Once again Jessica sang for her sisters. Excitedly they asked Jessica to try other words with the tune of "Good Morning to All" to see if the new notes fit many occasions.

"Try Happy Vacation to You," Patty said.

"Happy Journey," said Mary.

"Happy New Year. Happy Christmas," urged Mildred.

Jessica sang all their ideas.

"What would you like to hear, Mama?" Patty asked. Martha smiled at her daughters. Was it not so long ago Patty was a little girl with golden-red curls, and Jessica, the baby born with the morning? Each child was a song of life in her memory garden with William. "Try Happy Birthday," laughed Mama. So Jessica sang the famous little song in Louisville for the first time at 1109 Second Street.

Happy Birthday to you,
Happy Birthday to you,
Happy Birthday, dear children,
Happy Birthday to you.

Still the true test was in the kindergarten. The next day the song followed Patty and Mildred to school like Mary's Little Lamb. *These* notes the children learned with ease. Mildred fingered piano keys as the children's voices welcomed another day of play to Miss Patty's kindergarten. When the singing stopped they heard: "Eureeeeekkkka!" Patty and Mildred's song was finally born. One part words, one part melody, one part happy child.

And as soon as the first birthday celebration in school came along, well, you know the famous little song the children sang.

Footnote to History

If musical scales were train rails of time, you could ride along with the sisters' song to see what happened to it next, and why the train might be called The Birthday Mystery Express! In 1893 "Good Morning to All" was copyrighted in Patty and Mildred's *Song Stories for the Kindergarten*. At that time, "Happy Birthday to You" was not copyrighted on its own, but its words were sung to the Morning Greeting's melody in the Louisville kindergartens.

The same year as the copyright, the two songs, twins in melody, but not in words, traveled to the Chicago World's Fair, where visitors heard them at Patty's popular Kindergarten Exhibition. The songs chugged on to New York City in 1906 when Patty left Louisville to become a Professor at Columbia University's Teachers College. Her many kindergarten student-teachers, including her sister, Jessica, took the songs with them to classrooms near and far.

By the 1920s both songs had a loving home in the kindergarten, but "Happy Birthday" also traveled from the classroom, going into the world on its own. It went on radio. In 1924 the song went into Robert Coleman's song book, *Harvest Hymns*, printed (for the first time and without credit to the sisters) as the second verse to "Good Morning to All"!

Next, the Birthday Song became a Singing Telegram going into homes across America, but again without credit to the Hills. Without a proper copyright, few knew the history of the song, so a mystery grew. Was it a folk tune? Who wrote the words and put them to the melody?

Finally, the Birthday Song went to Broadway where Patty heard it in a musical written by a famous composer, Irving Berlin, as she sat in the audience! By now Jessica was furious.

She went to court to tell the world "Happy Birthday" was her *sisters'* gift to children.

On July 16, 1935 in New York City, Patty and Jessie, now white-haired professors, gave testimony as to how and when and who wrote "Happy Birthday to You"! Sadly, Mildred had died in 1916. Mary, Wallace, Archie, and Martha Hill were gone, too. Only Jessica and Patty remained to testify to lawyers, Mr. Stark and Mr. Pepper. Miss Gertrude Esterhaus took down their words under oath. First Jessica told Mr. Stark she recalled being fifteen, standing at the piano, and singing "Good Morning to All" and "Happy Birthday to You" for her sisters.

Patty told Mr. Stark she wrote the words to "Good Morning to All," and Mildred, the music. "I would take it

into the school and test it with the little children. And though only the words from "Good Morning to All" were put in the song book, we used the song for "Goodbye to You," "Happy Journey to You," "Happy Christmas to You," and so forth and so on."

Then Mr. Stark asked Patty the question to finally put all myth and mystery to rest. "Did you also use the words 'Happy Birthday to You'?"

One can imagine Patty's clear gaze giving him a wise look. For forty-three years children had come to her kindergarten, a land of promise, where no child stayed a stranger singing "Good Morning to All" and every child made a friend singing "Happy Birthday to You." Patty answered him with her knowing cap on and her head held as high as Bellewood's tower: "We certainly did with every birthday celebration in the school."

In 1935 "Happy Birthday to You" was copyrighted, giving credit to Patty and Mildred. Its copyright ends in 2030. If the song's melody and lyrics are commercially used together, a fee is paid to the Hill Foundation (to value early childhood education) and to its publisher, Warner-Chappell. "Happy Birthday" is reported to earn between one-million and two-million dollars a year, yet the sisters never composed the song for money. Its value was in celebrating the worth of each person born on this Earth, a lesson learned in their most unusual home.

A Note to the Reader

This story about the Hill family is based on real facts about them. It was said that the Hill family had one heart and eight minds. And perfect harmony! Mildred, the oldest, was the first to inherit her parents' love of music. Reverend Hill's music director at Bellewood was from Germany, and lucky Mildred studied under his instruction, and later with a teacher in Chicago. She was Music head of Louisville's Training School and a highly respected composer in many musical circles.

In Louisville, Patty followed Anna Bryan as the kindergarten principal. Patty was an exciting mind in the new field, because she studied the child while others studied Fredrick Froebel's system. She retired in 1935 as Professor Emeritus, Director of Columbia Teaching College.

Not surprisingly in an independent family, Patty, Mildred, Jessie, Mary, and Wallace never married. Only Archie did, and had a son. But Patty lived a life surrounded by children, serving education at a time when teachers spent afternoons in students' homes caring for the family to aid the child. Patty died in 1946 and some in tribute sang "Happy Birthday" at her Louisville grave.

Louisville is rightfully proud of its Hill Family and to being home to "Happy Birthday"! There is even a "Happy Birthday" parking lot in Louisville, where local lore says the sisters sang the song for the first time to the daughter of a friend in a historic cottage. Patty and Jessica said under oath the song originated in their home, tested in kindergarten, during the years 1889 and 1890. Their sworn words are now stored in Albany, New York— the proof of how a morning greeting was born in a garden and grew into the most played song in the world—"Happy Birthday to You"—by simply celebrating the happy child in everyone.

Thank you, dear sisters, for the song that never grows old and makes a birthday child feel as loved as the children playing in a magical room long ago . . . .